Motives

"Why Do I Do the Things I Do?"

Resources for Changing Lives

A Ministry of
THE CHRISTIAN COUNSELING AND
EDUCATIONAL FOUNDATION
Glenside, Pennsylvania

RCL Ministry Booklets
Susan Lutz, Series Editor

Motives

"Why Do I Do the Things I Do?"

Edward T. Welch

P&R PUBLISHING
P.O. BOX 817 • PHILLIPSBURG • NEW JERSEY 08865-0817

© 2003 by Edward T. Welch

All rights reserved. No part of this booklet may be reproduced, stored in a retrieval system, or transmitted in any form or by any means—electronic, mechanical, photocopy, recording, or otherwise—except for brief quotations for the purpose of review or comment, without the prior permission of the publisher, P&R Publishing Company, P.O. Box 817, Phillipsburg, New Jersey 08865-0817.

Scripture quotations are from the HOLY BIBLE, NEW INTERNATIONAL VERSION®. NIV®. Copyright © 1973, 1978, 1984 by International Bible Society. Used by permission of Zondervan Publishing House. All rights reserved.

Printed in the United States of America

Library of Congress Cataloging-in-Publication Data

Welch, Edward T., 1953–
    Motives : "Why do I do the things I do?" / Edward T. Welch.
        p. cm.—(Resources for changing lives)
    ISBN-10: 0-87552-692-6
    ISBN-13: 978-0-87552-692-8
    1. Motivation (Psychology)—Religious aspects—Christianity. 2. Christian life. I. Title. II. Series.

BV4599.5.M66 W45 2003
253.5'2—dc21
                        2002192690

People are complex. We've been compared to icebergs (with more under the surface than above it) and onions (with multiple layers). There is behavior that you see and motives that you don't. A colleague may appear to be very nice, when all the while he is using you to climb the corporate ladder. A friend may seem unresponsive when you share a painful story, but the truth is she is terrified of hurting you by saying the wrong thing. A football player might swagger around like the big man on campus, when beneath the bravado he is meekly carrying out his father's show-no-weakness policy. No one sees that he lives in fear of his father's unpredictable temper.

Our public actions tell one story; our private intentions can tell another. Behind the "what we do" of our lives—our words and actions—is the "why we do it"—our motives.

Chances are that you have considered some of the "whys" of your behavior.

Why didn't I ask for directions?
Why did I marry this person?

Why did I just bet my entire paycheck on a horse race?

And, every once in a while, even deeper questions come knocking.

Why am I alive? What is the purpose of my life? Or, more generally, *Why do I do what I do?*

These questions usually arise when we have regrets about something we've done. Otherwise, we tend to relegate them to the margins of our lives.

The purpose of this booklet is to consider more closely why we do the things we do.

Motives Are Important

Even though we don't always think about them, motives are important. They are the reason we like Robin Hood and loathe the Sheriff of Nottingham. Robin Hood may have been the outlaw, but we consider his motives noble.

If a husband is meeting his wife's best friend to get gift ideas for his wife, he is praised. But if his motive is to test the waters for a possible affair, he is a scoundrel.

Parents are not simply interested in mechanical or angry obedience from their children. They are concerned about a child's attitude, which is another name for motive. Parents care what children do—and why.

Or consider the realm of addictions. Whether it is food, sex, drugs, or alcohol, an addiction seems automatic. The addicted person has been taken captive. To ask why seems as silly as asking, "Why did you catch a cold?" But even here, motives are important. Beneath the addictive behavior are wants and desires. Addicts may be enslaved, but, at some level, they volunteer to be. They are motivated to continue their addiction because it gives them comfort, pleasure, power, temporary freedom from pain, revenge, autonomy, and so on. To ignore these possible motives is to leave people at the mercy of their addictive cravings. Even if they are abstinent or self-controlled, their efforts will not be enough to change their fundamental motivations.

In other words, motives are not only important, in many situations they *must* be revealed and changed. If our motives don't change, *we* won't change.

Sample Motives

A list of possible motivations would be endless, but there are a dozen or so that seem especially common. To discover the things that motivate you, ask yourself these questions: *What motivates me? Why do I do what I do?* Even better, ask, *What do I really want? If I don't have _____, I am miserable.* Here are some typical answers:

Pleasure	Power
Freedom/Autonomy	Peace
Love/Intimacy	Happiness
Significance/Reputation	Comfort
Respect/Admiration	Meaning
Control	Success

You have probably been motivated by all of these at one time or another, but some people have specialties.

- The man who is always late and unavailable when there is work to be done might be motivated by comfort.
- The wife who is mortified that a surprise visitor saw her messy house is motivated by reputation.
- The father whose children are fearful and whose wife is cautious wants power.
- The teen who chafes at any curfew wants freedom.

- The mother who never lets her children stay with a babysitter wants control.

To complicate the picture, there are often multiple motivations for a single behavior. The man who goes AWOL when there is work to be done might be lazy and driven by comfort, but he also might want respect, success, or meaning. He avoids work because he is afraid he will fail at the job and lose the respect of others.

Or consider the teen who wants to answer to no one but herself and grumbles whenever a parent asks her to do anything. Her inner life is not that simple. She may crave independence because others will think she is cool if she takes a stand against her parents. Perhaps she is driven by a desire for love, and she wants to be out with friends to increase her chances of finding a boyfriend. It is even possible that she is saying to her parents, "Can you still love me even when I am not perfect?"

God's Word and Motivation

At this point, we need more guidance. We know that motives are important, but we also know that the more we examine them, the more complex they become.

And what happens when we do see and understand some of our motives? Is insight going to help? Will insight alone change us?

We need Scripture to take us farther than we can take ourselves. Since motives are such an important part of life, we would expect God's Word to speak about them, and it certainly does. In fact, the entire Bible is a book about motivation.

It's All About the Heart

The key word is the *heart*. In Scripture, this is the source of all human motivation. The heart is the wellspring of life (Prov. 4:23), the root that determines whether the fruit of the tree will be good or bad (Jer. 17:5–8; Luke 6:43–45). It is our true self. Appearing nearly 1000 times in the Bible, *heart* can have a broad range of meaning, but at its core are our motivations. Simply put, the heart's root motivation is, "I WANT." "I want comfort, power, pleasure, control . . . for myself, against God." By nature, the heart is selfish. It wants what it wants when it wants it. It doesn't want God setting limits or providing direction. When changed by God himself, the heart's selfish and anti-God motives are not erased, but they are gradually replaced by a desire to love God and live for him alone.

At first, this description might not seem to fit your own experience. Life does not feel like it is always about God. Some people haven't even heard of the true God, so how can their behavior have anything to do with him? However, you don't have to be self-consciously thinking about God to be for or against him.

When a teen violates a parent's directions, it doesn't always feel like an act of rebellion against the parent. It just feels like the teen wanted to do what he or she wanted to do. The disobedience was "nothing personal," yet it *was* personal. It was a desire for freedom, and against the parent's authority.

Or take internet pornography. For many people, it feels like a little-less-than-innocent indulgence. It might not be honorable, but it doesn't feel like it's *against* anyone. No one is getting hurt, and it's just a small pleasure. But the reality goes deeper than that. People *are* hurt by it, and it *is* against the spouse. It breaks the vows once made to her, and is a temporary shifting of marital allegiance. The pornography lover is saying that his desires cannot be met through his spouse, so he can indulge in mental betrayal to find the satisfaction he craves. Going even deeper into the heart, such behavior is against God. These actions say that God is either blind or far away. After all, who would do such a thing if he believed he was in the presence of the King? The pornography lover is implicitly saying that God is just a person, limited in what he does and where he can be. Furthermore, when God says, "Be holy as I am holy," the pornography lover responds by saying "No" or "Later." He responds to the King's command to pursue sexual purity as if it were a mere suggestion.

These examples illustrate the fact that all of life is personal. Whether we consciously think about it or not, we know *the* God (Rom. 1:21), the Searcher of hearts (Jer. 17:10). We don't just have a fuzzy idea that there is a god or a "higher power." The Bible says that in our hearts, we have a personal knowledge of the God who truly is. The problem is that we don't always like his intrusive or disruptive ways, and we try to ignore or avoid him. We "suppress the truth" we know (Rom. 1:18–21).

But we are not always blind to these motives. When we are going through especially hard times, our God-motives often come to the surface. We may find ourselves saying, "God, what did I ever do to deserve this? How could you do this to me?" The tough times expose our basic allegiances. Do we live for God or for ourselves?

Even with atheists, the God-ward heart will be revealed. Atheists might live with a profound fear of death, revealing that, at some level, they know they will someday face the living God. Or they might consult palm readers for direction, tacitly acknowledging a divine plan and their fear that it might not go well for them. These behaviors are echoes of God-oriented motivations. In their hearts is the question, *Will I live independent of God or will I acknowledge him as Lord?*

Granted, we are not always aware of these motives, but that doesn't mean they don't exist. *All* of our motives are hard to see.

Consider the case of the ancient Israelites. In Numbers 14 they had just seen unparalleled miracles performed by the God who had chosen them as his very own people. After leading them out of slavery in Egypt and destroying Pharaoh's army, God provided them with a new and fertile land. The problem was that the people living in the land thought it was theirs, and they weren't going to give it up without a fight.

The spies who scouted the land came back with a mixed report: the land was ideal, but the people in it were powerful. At this news, the people started complaining and grumbling. "That night all the people of the community raised their voices and wept aloud. All the Israelites grumbled against Moses and Aaron, and the whole assembly said to them, 'If only we had died in . . . this desert'" (Num. 14:1–2).

In this case, the complaint seems legitimate. Moses and Aaron had led Israel to a land filled with mighty warriors, and the people were more familiar with making bricks than waging war. Who wouldn't grumble? Their motivation was simple: they wanted to live! They reasoned that life, even in slavery, was better than death, and with that most of us would agree. This was why they were grumbling against Moses and Aaron.

But their motivations were deeper than that.

"The Lord said to Moses, 'How long will these people treat me with contempt? . . . How long shall this wicked community grumble against me?'" (Num. 14:11, 27)

There it is, the heart's ever-present question: "Whom will you follow, worship, and trust?"

The people were complaining against God. God himself was their leader, their Father, the One who promised them the land and would lead them into battle. He had already defeated the Egyptians without one Israelite raising a sword. He had already been taking care of their daily needs. In that context, the *why* of Israel's complaining had everything to do with God. As Moses had pointed out in an earlier episode, "You are not grumbling against us, but against the LORD" (Ex. 16: 8).

We can paraphrase the motives behind their grumbling this way: "God, we don't think you are powerful. We don't think you are good. You haven't given us everything we want when we want it." Their motives were against God.

The event can be charted like this.

Our circumstances
(*The difficulties of the desert*)

Our words and deeds
(*Complaining and grumbling*)

Our surface motives—personal desires,
such as significance, security, or love
(*We want to live in Egypt rather
than die in the desert.*)

Our deeper motives—are we for self or for others?
(*How dare Moses not give us what we want?*)

Our deepest motives—are we for self or for God?
(*We are angry with God.*)

Idols of the Heart

- Whom do you love (Deut. 6:5; 1 John 2:15)—the world or Jesus?
- Whom do you trust (Jer. 17:5–8)—people or the true God?
- Whom (or what) do you worship (2 Kings 17:36)—idols or God?
- Whom will you serve (Matt. 6:24)—money or God?
- Whom do you obey (1 John 3:10)—the Devil or God?
- For whose glory do you live (Rom. 1:21–23)—your own or God's?
- Where is your treasure (Matt. 6:21)—in the world or in Christ?
- To whom do you belong (John 8:44)—the Devil or God?

The heart is always asking these questions. At the most basic level, we are either for God or against him.

In Scripture, the most common way of describing this choice is through the question, Whom will you worship? The choice is either the true God or idols. The entire history of Israel was the conflict between the two (Ex. 20:2–6; 1 Kings 11:9–11; 19:10). All sin was summarized as idolatry (Deut. 4:23). Although this language sounds old-fashioned to us, what motivates our hearts today is no different. A quick survey of our hearts will most likely reveal age-old idols.

The most transparent illustration of modern idolatry is drug or alcohol addiction. Go to any AA meeting and you will hear the language of idolatry spoken:

> Before I was sober, nothing came between me and my booze. Booze was my spouse and my best friend. It was priority number one. It was my life. I worshipped it.

The bottle or my kids? This is a matter of allegiances and worship. You can almost see the addict taking the beloved idol and bowing down to it, asking it to bless the day and bring increased boldness or freedom from pain.

On the surface, the addict is motivated by the pleasure he takes in his drug. One step deeper, it is easy to see that his allegiance is more personal—it is against his spouse and his children, and for his drug. Yet the allegiances go deeper still. Will it be God or idols? Whom will he worship? The idol in this case is a bottle of booze. But even the alcohol is not the major problem. The problem, of course, is us. The problem resides in our hearts.

Idols are the way we try to satisfy our hearts' desires. Booze is a means to get what we want. So is money. Even people can be our objects of worship because they can give us the power, love, or respect we crave. All idols are objects of the heart's self-centered affections (Ezek. 14:3). Whatever we trust in or love is an idol if it is not the true God.

Now go back to the list of possible motives.

Pleasure	Power
Freedom/Autonomy	Peace
Love/Intimacy	Happiness
Significance/Reputation	Comfort
Respect/Admiration	Meaning
Control	Success

Most of these are not bad in themselves, but when we value them more than God, they become idols. The problem is not so much that we want these things, but that we want them too much. They become our goal, our hope, our purpose. We feel like we need them. When they are out of reach, life seems meaningless.

Ask yourself the following questions to see

if some of the deeper motives of your heart begin to emerge.

- What are the times when life doesn't seem worth living?
- What do you love? What do you hate? What do you hope for, want, crave?
- What is your goal? What are your dreams or fantasies?
- What do you fear? What do you worry about?
- What do you feel you need? Where do you find refuge, comfort, pleasure, or security?
- What defines success or failure for you?
- When do you say, "If only . . ." ("If only my husband would . . .")?
- Where do you believe that God has let you down?
- When have you struggled with bitterness or jealousy? What are you saying you want?
- What does money mean to you? (Notice how money can temporarily satisfy each of these desires.)
- When do you get depressed (because your idol has let you down)?
- What do you see as your rights? When do you get angry?

"I just feel rage," Steve said, looking like an overheated car. "Every time the guy in the next office walks by me, he shoots me a condescending look. I can understand why people murder."

Steve is angry and controlled by this other person. That's obvious. But *why* is he angry? Chances are that Steve's anger has something to do with his worship. Perhaps he worships at the altar of respect, and he has not been given the respect he demands. As a result, he is against his co-worker. He has declared war! But even more, he is against God, resisting the fact that God uses difficult people to refine us. Instead of submitting to God's sovereign decisions and learning to forgive and love, Steve is saying, "I will be God, at least in this case." His desires rule.

Here is a general principle: your attitude toward God will be revealed in your worst human relationship. If you hate someone, you are ultimately hating God. If you don't forgive, you are usurping God's authority to act as judge.

Why Idols?

Steve's case offers a glimpse of the behind-the-scenes motives of idolatry. He reminds us that no one has to be taught idolatry: we figure it out all by ourselves. Like ancient Israel, we have front row seats to the power and glory of God. We are told explicitly by God not to worship idols, yet we too make our version of a golden calf (Ex. 32). What drives us to do this? As creatures, we are designed to trust in something beyond ourselves. But why do we trust in things that don't seem to merit our trust?

Be warned. The answers aren't pretty, but they apply to us all.

We are proud. Isaiah 2:6–22 reveals that idolaters are arrogant. Idolaters, even when they are bowing down, are "arrogant," "proud," and "lofty." Apparently, our idols are actually intended to exalt ourselves and our own desires. Even in our idolatry we want nothing above ourselves. We choose idols in part because we believe they can give us what we want. The god of drugs brings fearlessness, the god of sex promises pleasure, the god of wealth holds out power and influence. Like the prophets of Baal, we are arrogant enough to believe that we can manipulate the idol—whether by self-mutilation or some other means—so it will serve us.

We crave autonomy. Autonomy means that we call the shots. Idolaters want to make the rules rather than submit to the lordship of the living God. This was the essence of Adam's original sin. Even though God had clearly spoken, Adam wanted to devise his own guidelines. In idolatry, we want to establish our own parallel universe, separate from God's.

We want to indulge our desires. Both pride and autonomy point to the fact that we are creatures who want something. We want *more* (Eph. 4:19). Idolatry was typically associated with orgies, drunkenness, and other forms of self-indulgence (Ex. 32; 1 Cor. 10:7). It is covetousness and greed (Eph. 5:5). In the New Testament, *desire* is cautioned against throughout.

> So I say, live by the Spirit, and you will not gratify the desires (*epithumia*) of the sinful nature. (Gal. 5:16)

> All of us also lived among them at one time, gratifying the cravings of our sinful nature and following its desires and thoughts. (Eph. 2:3)

> Having lost all sensitivity, they have given themselves over to sensuality so as

to indulge in every kind of impurity, with a continual lust for more. (Eph. 4:19)

Each one is tempted when, by his own evil desire, he is dragged away and enticed. (James 1:14)

Dear friends, I urge you, as aliens and strangers in the world, to abstain from sinful desires, which war against your soul. (1 Peter 2:11)

These verses remind us again that "I WANT" is the song of the human heart. In it there is arrogance, autonomy, and unrestrained desire. Idolatry is about me—my desires, my wants. My purpose is not to exalt the idol above myself, but to use the idol to give me what I want. When I am afraid, I look to the idol of money to give me security. I don't want money to rule me; I want to use it to get what I want. When I want pleasure, I cling to the idols of sex, food, or sleep. The problem is that I never quite feel like I have enough. So I want more.

This is why idols multiply. Our desires are insatiable. When we place our trust in idols, we find that they cannot satisfy our desires or sustain our hopes. So we look for even more. The multiplication of gods in Greek mythology or Hinduism depicts what goes on in our hearts every day. The heart is, indeed, an idol factory.

Idols and Christians

All this talk about lurking idols seems foreign to many Christians. After all, we don't have idols in our homes, and we have already sworn allegiance to Jesus Christ. Don't forget, however, that idolatry quietly resides in every heart. Christians are not sinless yet; that will only happen when Jesus Christ returns. In the meantime, we battle, especially at the level of our motivations and imaginations. The warnings against idolatry and hypocrisy are rightly directed to us.

Christian idolatry is more subtle than an outright, vocal abandonment of Christ. We may simply feel like Christ is not enough. We reason, *He can be counted on for eternal salvation but will he really give me the things I feel I need, like money, marriage, or personal pleasure?* So, just to be safe, we spread our trust between the true God and various idols. It's like having a diversified stock portfolio. We cheat on our taxes, excuse our premarital sexual relationships, and avoid inconvenient people. It doesn't seem so bad because we haven't actually renounced Christ, but this compromised trust is equivalent to turning away from God.

Change from the Heart

When we face this fact, all we can do is say, "OK, I give up. 'The heart is deceitful above all things and beyond cure' (Jer. 17:9). Guilty as charged." Now what? Do we simply wait for Christ to return, or is there something we can do now?

The answer, of course, is that we begin the fight against sin immediately. All Scripture points to this, and the fact that the Father has sent us the Holy Spirit indicates that we have more ammunition than we need. But how do we go about it?

We Consider Our Hearts. The path of change always goes through the heart. We look at the fruit of our lives—the big and little sins, the anxieties and fears, the disappointments and despair—and ask what they tell us about our relationship with God. We ask ourselves those revealing questions: *What did I want?*

What do I believe? How is this against other people? In what do I trust? What am I saying about God?

If we see sexual sin, our hearts are full of wants. We believe that God is not good and doesn't really see our private lives. We trust in our own devices to find satisfaction.

If we see jealousy, our hearts believe that life can be found in what other people have. Furthermore, not only do we want it, we wish *they* didn't have it. We see God as our errand boy who has not given us what we wanted or deserved.

If we see disrespect of authority, our hearts are saying that we want nothing above ourselves: not parents, not a boss, not God.

If children are fighting over a toy, change does *not* come by discovering who had it first. Instead, change begins when children admit that fights and quarrels come from "your desires that battle within you."

> You want something but don't get it. . . . You do not have, because you do not ask God. When you ask, you do not receive, because you ask with wrong motives, that you may spend what you get on your pleasures. You adulterous people, don't you know that friendship

with the world is hatred toward God? (James 4:2–4)

To omit this step is to nurture Pharisees who look good on the outside but whose "hearts are far from me" (Matt. 15:8). We all can do the right thing to protect our reputations, but God wants more. He doesn't want sacrifices and offerings that make us look good in front of others. "The sacrifices of God are a broken spirit; a broken and contrite heart, O God, you will not despise" (Ps. 51:17).

We Turn and Know the Triune God. Having looked at our hearts, we turn to Jesus. True change takes place when we focus on knowing the One who truly deserves our worship (2 Peter 1:3). Though many of us assume that change involves a plan with a series of steps, change on the heart level centers on knowing a person.

This is true even on a human level. If you think about the things that have led to change in your life, you will probably find that people were usually the catalyst. Perhaps it was a person's presence during a difficult time, a word of encouragement when you felt like a misfit, a friend who stayed closer than a brother, a spouse's gentle rebuke, or a person whose character and life were inspirational. People change us. How much more should we expect God to change us!

That is why the path of change goes through the heart and continues on to the gospel, where God chose to most fully reveal himself in the death and resurrection of Christ. It is in Jesus that the Father ultimately displays his goodness, his power, and his glory. And it is in Jesus that we find the power to change.

When you come to Jesus, expect to be surprised. You can't be changed by someone ordinary. Having seen a little of our heart's motives, start by being surprised that Jesus accepts and forgives all who come to him. This is what the cross ensures. There is no work of penance required, no "going to the woodshed for a licking," no sitting in the time out chair. Instead, forgiveness of sins comes from God. It is received as a gift through faith (Rom. 1:17). If forgiveness came by anything we did, it would detract from the glory of what Christ did. It would make God's forgiveness ordinary. It would be no different from the way we forgive people who repay us for what they have done. But divine forgiveness is like nothing you have ever experienced. It was extended to us *while* we were sinners against God, not simply after we tried to reform ourselves. Given this jaw-dropping love, we can "approach the throne of grace with confidence" (Heb. 4:16). And this is just the beginning. This love also changes the way we respond to the circumstances of life.

Do you complain and grumble? Now you know that it is against God. Now you affirm that he is generous and gives in abundance.

Do you indulge in sins you think are hidden? Now you know that these are against God. You acknowledge that the Revealer of hearts is the One who sees all of his creation at all times (Ps. 139). What's more, you thank him for forgiving and liberating you from the slavery of sin.

Do you struggle with fear? Now you know that he will never leave you or forsake you. You affirm that he is good.

Do you want to be the one to call the shots in your own life, at least in one area? Like Adam, you must think that there is life apart from the Life giver. But now, look at the cross again. Doesn't it prove his goodness and his great love for you? How can you think that, after giving his own Son, he will be stingy with you now?

The power to change comes as we know God. So seek him. Ask others to teach you about him. Pray that you would know him. If you do, you *will* know him because God delights in revealing himself to us.

> I keep asking that the God of our Lord Jesus Christ, the glorious Father, may give you the Spirit of wisdom and revelation, so that you may know him better. (Eph. 1:17)

> I pray that you, being rooted and established in love, may have power, together with all the saints, to grasp how wide and long and high and deep is the love of Christ, and to know this love that surpasses knowledge—that you may be filled to the measure of all the fullness of God. (Eph 3:17–19)

We Trust and Obey. A growing knowledge of a spouse or friend often leads us to acts of love. In a similar way, our personal knowledge of God compels us into action. It leads us to trust and obey.

The pattern of Scripture is clear. Its many stories reveal our hearts and then point us to the God who forgives, woos, judges, initiates, and pursues. After seeing who God is and what he has done, we find a "therefore."

> Be imitators of God, therefore, as dearly loved children and live a life of love, just as Christ loved us and gave himself up for us as a fragrant offering and sacrifice to God. (Eph. 5:1–2)

Once we know him we will *want* to follow him. Having been loved so much, we will want to know how to love him back. Everything that follows the "therefore" is God's explanation of how to do that.

We love him, for example, by putting off falsehood and speaking truthfully (Eph. 4:25), not sinning in our anger (Eph. 4:26), forgiving others as we have been forgiven (Luke 7:36–50), working rather than stealing (Eph. 4:28), loving friends and enemies (Rom. 12:9–21), being content in all our circumstances (Phil. 4:12), fighting the battle of self-control, and growing in patience, gentleness, and joy (Gal. 5:23). In all these ways, we love and honor our Heavenly Father.

People are indeed complex. Beneath the surface of life is a heart that is always on the move, looking for objects in which to trust (Luke 24:25; Rom. 10:10). The heart has purposes (Prov. 20:5; Dan. 1:8), inclinations (Eccl. 10:2), intents (Heb. 4:12), imaginations and schemes (Prov. 6:18), desires (Ps. 10:3; James 4:1), and cravings and lusts (1 John 2:16; Eph. 4:19). It is not surprising that, with such complexity, our hearts are not always immediately understandable to others or even ourselves (Matt. 15:8; 1 Cor. 4:5; Prov. 16:2; Jer. 17:9). Like the bottom of a well or the roots of trees, our hearts tend to be hidden, and we can never fully know their depths.

But you don't have to be a master analyst. All you need is a willingness to say, "Search me, O God" (Ps. 139:23), and you will begin to see.

Don't be too concerned if you feel like you are just scratching the surface. More important than knowing your motives is knowing God, and God is very generous in revealing himself. He should be your primary focus. We should be spending more time looking at Christ than inspecting our own hearts. Because if you are growing in the knowledge of God, you will be changed—even to the depths of your heart.

Edward T. Welch directs the School of Biblical Counseling at the Christian Counseling and Educational Foundation in Glenside, Pennsylvania, where he is a counselor and faculty member.

RCL Ministry Booklets

Booklets by Jeffrey S. Black, Michael R. Emlet, Walter Henegar, Robert D. Jones, Susan Lutz, James C. Petty, David Powlison, Paul David Tripp, Edward T. Welch, and John Yenchko.

ADD
Anger
Angry at God?
Bad Memories
Depression
Forgiveness
God's Love
Guidance
Homosexuality
"Just One More"
Marriage
Motives
OCD
Pornography

Pre-Engagement
Priorities
Procrastination
Prodigal Children
Self-Injury
Sexual Sin
Stress
Suffering
Suicide
Teens and Sex
Thankfulness
Why Me?
Why Worry?
Worry

See all the books and booklets in the Resources for Changing Lives series at www.prpbooks.com